# He is Always
# Faithful

*Finding Peace in the Midst of Heartache and Disappointment*

ISBN 978-1-952320-18-7 (Paperback)
*He is Always Faithful: Finding Peace in the Midst of Heartache and Disappointment*
Copyright © 2020 by Wanda S. Hudson

All rights reserved.

No part of this publication may be reproduced, distributed, or transmitted in any form or by any means, including photocopying, recording, or other electronic or mechanical methods, without the prior written permission of the publisher, except in the case of brief quotations embodied in critical reviews and certain other noncommercial uses permitted by copyright law.

Bible verses used from the following translations: *Christian Standard Bible; New American Standard; The Message; New Kings James; New International Version*

For permission requests, write to the publisher at the address below.

Yorkshire Publishing
4613 E. 91st St,
Tulsa, OK 74137
www.YorkshirePublishing.com
918.394.2665

Printed in the USA

# *He is Always*
# *Faithful*

*Finding Peace in the Midst of Heartache and Disappointment*

## Wanda S. Hudson

TULSA

## *Dedication*

To Zack and Charlyanne: Thank you so much for your love and support. You both have been my counselors, confidants, first readers of my book, and most importantly, my prayer partners. Thank you for giving me the privilege of being Grandma Hudson to my five wonderful grandkids, Andrew, Karah, Philip, Rebekah, and Nathan.

# *Acknowledgements*

This book would not have been possible without the encouragement of my friends and family. When I first began telling people I was writing a book, so many of you were my cheerleaders. I heard comments like: "I can't wait to read your book" or, "That is amazing, let me know when you are finished." Or my favorite: " I want a signed copy."

Thanks to so many of you who sent me encouraging messages on Facebook or by text asking when my book will be ready and that you are so proud of me for writing a book.

To my family:

Eric and Sarah—Thank you for your love and encouragement. It was fun making the moving trips with you. I appreciate all your help.

To my nieces Lisa and Misty and their families:

You are both more like daughters to me than nieces. Your love and support has helped me so much.

To my sisters Sonya, Ellen, and Tiffany and their families:

Thank you for your love and support. I appreciate your acceptance of my story.

To Doug and his family:

Thank you for reaching out and finding me. I am grateful for our time together.

A huge shout out to Melody Box. She has been my constant encourager. I once texted her when I was having doubts. I asked her, what made me think I could write a book? She told me I have a story to tell and there are people who need to hear my story of God's love, forgiveness and grace. She went on to tell me I am a great writer. She was one of my readers.

My church family has been a constant support throughout this process. It is a privilege and honor to serve our Heavenly Father with you all. I hold my Sunday School Class, Ruth's Open Door, so close to my heart. Thank you for your listening ears, loving hearts, and constant prayers.

My Freedom School Family showed me nothing but grace and love upon hearing my story. I appreciate the kindness and acceptance. It has been an honor to teach at the best school in Oklahoma with the best kids in Oklahoma!

My birthday club girls have been with me for over twenty five years. Words cannot express the way you have loved me over those years. I treasure all our good times, especially the laughs. You girls are the best!

This book would not be possible without my loving, heavenly Father. He saved me and freed me to become the person I was meant to be by His love, grace, and mercy. Everything that has happened in my story was in His perfect timing. His healing has brought real peace in my life. He is always faithful.

# *Praises for He is Always Faithful*

Wanda Hudson has been a blessing in my life for several decades. I have had the privilege of watching her consistent ministry of prayer and encouragement impact many lives for the kingdom of God. I am honored to be her pastor and serve with her family in our church. Wanda's story is one that is courageous and painful, yet marked by faithfulness. This book will be a significant inspiration to you!

Dr. Eric Costanzo
Pastor, South Tulsa Baptist Church

Wanda has put God's grace and mercy in this book! She took a difficult time in her life and bared her soul to openly help others. As I walked this journey with her, I have seen the changes God has made in her life. Whether you have placed a child for adoption, experienced the death of a child or similar life crisis, I recommend you read this book. You will see and feel the power of God.

Regina Smith
College friend

Wanda and I have been friends for over twenty-five years. One thing I admire about Wanda is that she speaks from her heart. Her writing reflects her heart.

Barbara Howerton
Birthday Club Member

*Wanda S. Hudson*

He Is Always Faithful is an outpouring of hope for anyone longing to overcome feelings of loneliness, remorse, sadness, or grief. Wanda's story, while tragic, is by no means a story of despair leaving you hopeless; instead you will read of God's faithfulness and God's providence on every page of this book. Her transparent and authentic writing style will draw you in and soon you will want to call her your dear friend. Be prepared to be inspired, encouraged, restored, and overwhelmed with the knowledge that God is faithful. He will never leave you. You can find the peace you search for in Him. What a privilege to call Wanda Hudson my lifelong friend and to be personally encouraged by her faith and walk with the Lord.

Melody Box<br>Author of He Can Be Trusted

# *Foreword*

It takes a lot of courage to share your story. Our stories are not perfect. They often come with regrets and mistakes followed by an array of emotions. These emotions can be uncomfortable to share. When we are candid with our past, it can not only bring great healing to ourselves but to others as well. That's the beauty of life. We are all on a journey. We are all living out our story. We have a choice to make as to what we will do with the time we are given on earth.

I am proud of my mom for taking a big step in sharing part of her journey with you. Her story reveals how to find hope in the midst of great trial, especially in dealing with regret and living with mistakes from her past. Her journey reveals the forgiveness and redemption that can only be found in a relationship with a faithful God who never gives up and is always there for us.

One of the best things we can do is learn from our past. Adoption can be a wonderful experience for a family who is unable to have children and have felt led to bring a child into their home. More time should be spent helping the mother who had to make the difficult decision to place her child for adoption. On the following pages, you will see a mother who struggled with that decision and how she found healing in a right relationship with God through Jesus Christ.

I am thankful that even though my mom lived with regrets and what ifs, it did not stop her from being the mom she needed to be for me. She was also a great elementary school teacher during this process. I always enjoyed hearing stories of students who would often tell her that she was one of their favorite teachers.

My mom is a remarkable person. One of the things I love most about her is how encouraging she is to me and to others. As you read this book, I hope you not only see the presence of God at work but realize this is not something reserved for certain people. We can all find forgiveness and hope in walking with Christ. In Philippians, Paul writes that nothing compares with the knowledge of knowing Christ personally. Paul says that everything he had believed to be gain was now considered loss because of Christ. My mom lived out this example in our home. She showed the importance of prayer and reading the Bible. We have always been part of a wonderful church family, which is so important. My family and I enjoy being part of that church family with her.

I am currently on a fourteen hour flight home from Asia, where I spent the last week ministering and working with people in that area. If it was not for my mom's example growing up, I would not be that person, following Christ with the hope He brings. Perhaps you are like my mom. We all are in a way. We have been living our lives one way up until this very point. Maybe it is time for you to consider making a change for the better in your life. David asks God in Psalm 139 to search him and reveal anything that isn't worthy.

> *Psalm 139:23-24 Search me, God, and know my heart; test me and know my concerns. See if there is any offensive way in me; lead me in the everlasting way.*

As you read through these pages, I pray that you would allow God to search your heart. Keep in mind that you too can find hope and forgiveness from God. Perhaps one day you will have the courage to share your journey with others.

Zack Hudson<br>
Associate Pastor<br>
South Tulsa Baptist Church

# *Please Read—Don't Miss This Part!!*

I am on the plane to North Carolina to see him. It has been forty years since we have been together. I am anxious to see him. What will he think? Will I meet his expectations or fall short? Will I be satisfied that I made this decision to see him? Has it just been too long? Am I kidding myself thinking this reunion will work? Why does he want to see me after all these years? Has he even thought about me over the years? Forty years without any communication at all. Not a letter, a phone call, or text. I have had no information at all. Now I will be with him in a few hours.

We were together for less than a year, yet we were totally connected, inseparable. I felt his every move. We were together every day. I loved him from day one. I had never experienced such love, never knew I could love someone this much. I still have the same deep love for him forty years later. Will it be enough? How does he feel? Will he be able to express his emotions to me? Will I be able to talk to him? Will he be a stranger to me?

The day we were separated is burned in my mind forever. It was so painful. The room was dark and a bit scary. He was with me and then they whisked him away. I wanted just a glimpse of him. When I close my eyes, I see the only real picture I have carried in my mind all these years. I see the curve of his small back but nothing more. It is burned in my memory forever.

Three days later, I went home alone. He was gone. I wanted to know where he was and who was with him. How could they love him as much as I do? Will we ever be together again? Is it really over? Questions that could never be answered. He was no longer mine and would never be again. I knew I would never see him again. I had no right to him and was no longer a part of his life. Someone else took my place. It's maddening how I can just go on with life. Part of me is gone, as if I lost a limb I will never get back. It's almost as if he never existed. It does not seem real. Was he really a part of me? Did the past year even happen?

My decision separated us forever. A decision I questioned over the years much more than I probably should have. A decision I should have never had to make. A decision that I buried inside of me for so many years but now has come to light.

\* \* \* \* \* \* \*

I pray you will be blessed by my story. Some specifics of my story will remain unwritten. There are many people involved, so out of respect for them and their families, I intentionally left out details that were not important to my story. Some of the people in my story are very private people, and I want to respect them. I can't and won't try to speak for them. I don't assume I know their hearts well enough to speak for them. They may want to share their story in the future. That will be their story to tell and not mine.

We all see things according to our perspective, and what I see and perceive may be much different than someone else's mindset. My situation is more difficult and painful for me because of the forty plus years I have experienced. I doubt anyone else would see it as I do given my experience. As I was writing, I prayed earnestly for God's guidance and direction. I asked Him to show me what to include, and to pray for hearts to understand why I am telling my story.

I hope you will be encouraged as you read. I know there are people who need to hear my story of God's mercy and grace. We experience various difficulties, disappointments, heartache, and pain in life. I want you to know there is hope in the midst of any tragedy. God can and will deliver you. He will always be with you. He loves you. He is faithful. The reason for sharing my story is as a testimony to God's faithfulness.

> ***2 Timothy 2:13*** *If we are faithless, He remains faithful, for He cannot deny Himself.*
>
> ***2 Thessalonians 3:3*** *The Lord is faithful, and He will strengthen you and guard you from the evil one.*

CHAPTER 1

# *Freedom*

I was thrilled to begin my freshman year of college. I was the first in my family to attend college. I wanted to succeed and make my family proud. I was also glad to be on my own. My parents were strict, and I wanted some freedom. I was away from home and lived on campus, which made me seem removed from my parents. I liked being on my own.

I met Robert at a welcome dance at the beginning of the semester. We really connected. He was a senior and not in any of my classes. During the dance, I could sense someone was watching me from across the room. It took him awhile to come over and ask me to dance. I know it sounds corny to say it was magic, but that is how it felt. It was an instant attraction. When he held my hand, I definitely felt sparks. I had never felt such a strong attraction. I could tell by the way he looked at me that he felt it too. This was new to me. I had never been in a serious relationship. I did not expect to feel this strongly so quickly. I did not date much in high school because my parents were so strict. I got to college never having had a serious relationship, not even a serious boyfriend in high school.

We sat at the dance and talked for a long time. He wanted to take me for a ride in his new car but I said no. I hardly knew him. He was very polite and not upset that I said no. He walked me back to the dorm. We made a date for the following night.

During the next three months we spent lots of time together. We studied, talked, went out to dinner, to the movies, and took many long walks. We would sit outside and talk for hours. We discussed many things. It really was perfect. We were so connected. I felt like I had known him much longer than a few months. I felt very safe, protected, and comfortable with Robert. I wanted to just hold onto him and never let go.

Robert told me that he had been engaged during his sophomore year. It was a bad break up. He discovered she was cheating. He was really hurt. He said he would never get serious about anyone for a very long time. I understood that. Marriage was not something I really thought about much.

I really felt like he was the one. I was cautious about talking to him because of his past. I did not want to scare him away. One night at dinner, he surprised me by asking if I ever thought about being married. He said he knew he told me that he did not want to get married but being with me had changed his mind. He told me he loved me and wanted to be with me forever. I was in love and it felt absolutely perfect. He did not ask me to marry him that night but there was no reason to rush. I knew we would be together forever.

One evening in early November, we went to dinner at an expensive out of town restaurant. Robert was nervous and seemed anxious. He did not eat much of his dinner. I was getting a bit panicky. Finally I got up the nerve to ask if something was wrong. He seemed surprised and said of course not. I don't think he realized how he was acting. He just could not seem to settle down.

We got in the car and headed home. He was very quiet. I was about to cry. We were almost home when he pulled off the side of the road. Was he going to let me out?

He started to cry. I was really scared. He took my hand. He told me he loved me. He said he wanted me in his life for always. He said that his feelings were so strong that it scared him. That made me feel a bit better since he had been acting strangely. He put his hand in his pocket and pulled out a small box.

He asked me to marry him right there on the side of the road. It was unbelievable. I said yes! We made plans to get married the following summer. Robert made me feel safe and protected. I knew he was the one for me. No one had ever given me so much attention and love. When we held hands, we were so connected. It was like we were one. Just the way he said my name made me smile. My life was getting settled. I was ecstatic.

Robert was a true gentleman. We did not even kiss until the third date. He was the whole package. It was my dream come true, except for the glass slipper!

My friends were skeptical when I shared my news. I know it was because Robert and I had only been together a few months. It's hard to explain that it seemed like we had been together much longer and were meant to be together. They also knew he had been engaged two years before. But the breakup was not his fault. I wanted them to be happy for me. It was upsetting that I did not have their support. I wondered if they saw something that I did not see.

I did not tell my parents because I knew how they would react. They would tell me that it was too soon. My parents did not even know I was dating Robert and that it was a serious relationship. I had also been detaching myself from my parents. I loved them but I was out from their supervision and on my own. My Dad was just too stern and controlling. I had better plans for myself.

I was not a Christian so I was not even aware of God and how He could affect my life. I was making plans for myself without regard to what God's plan was for me. When we are in control of our lives, they are really out of control. I thought I knew what was best for me.

*Isaiah 46:4 I have made you. I will carry you; I will sustain you and I will rescue you.*

CHAPTER 2

# *Is Robert the One?*

The college campus closed for Christmas break. Robert was from another town and went home. We managed to see each other some but not enough. I missed him so much. It was a long three weeks.

When classes resumed in January, we all moved back into the dorms. I was excited to be back on campus with Robert. He seemed different somehow. I asked him several times if something was wrong. He said no but was not very convincing. He was quiet and withdrawn, unlike before when we talked about everything. Before the break, we were together every day. Now it was a few times a week. He said he had to study a lot since it was his last semester. That seemed like a good reason, but still I questioned that. I was really scared. I thought something must have happened over the break. Did he like it better when we weren't together so much? Did he run into an old girlfriend back home? Did his parents not agree with him being engaged? He never talked about them. He never said anything about introducing me to them. We had never discussed that but I thought it would happen eventually. I thought it was strange that he did not talk about them. I decided he must not be close to them. That should have been a big warning sign, but I ignored it. I loved him and knew we would be together for the rest of our lives. I believed things would work themselves out. Our love will fix everything, right?

I need to mention here that Robert was from a very affluent background. He did not talk much about his parents, but I assumed they must have been wealthy by the way Robert dressed and the car he drove. My background was very different. I did not own a car and had to work while in college. My parents went to college but did not graduate with a degree. They both worked hard their whole lives. We lived very simply, and many would consider us poor. I had five siblings, and life was strenuous. I had one pair of shoes at a time and had maybe five sets of clothing. That may explain my love of shoes today! His parents were more than likely not agreeable because of my background or he may have not even mentioned me to them. I asked about them, but he never seemed to want to talk about them. As I mentioned before, he became very withdrawn.

I was not a Christian at this time, so I did not pray and seek His guidance. As I write this today, I have been a Christian for over forty years. It seems foreign to me that I was that girl. I was someone who just lived day by day without any regard to the Father. I made decisions by myself and thought I knew what was best for me. Decisions without God's guidance are disastrous.

At the beginning of February, Robert told me he did not want to get married. I did not see that coming. I was stunned. I just knew we would be together forever. I was still hopeful that things would work out and be fine. When I think about this today, I see how naive I was. There were clearly warning signs but when you want something so badly, you choose to ignore them.

Robert said he could never trust me like he should even though I had done nothing to make him suspicious. He blamed this on his past relationship. He told me he was sure I would eventually get tired of him and find someone else. I felt like he was hiding something. I felt like this was an excuse and not the real reason he did not want to marry me. When you are as close as we were, you can just tell. He would not talk and insisted that was the reason. It was heartbreaking. So much for things working themselves out.

I felt like I was in a fog. I was just going through the motions of going to class and trying to stay alive. I avoided places on campus where I knew I might run into Robert.

My friends were really supportive during this time. I am so glad they did not say, 'Told you so!'

One evening, I came home from the movies with my friends to find Robert sitting on the steps of my dorm. I had not seen him since our breakup which had been about three weeks. He had flowers and sure looked like he had been crying. He asked if he could talk to me. I sat down by him. He said he was sorry and really missed me. He said he did not like being without me. Would I consider getting back together? I was a naive young girl and really loved this guy. I did not want to live without him. I said yes.

Our wedding plans were back on but it just never felt right. I questioned my trust for him. He still did not want to talk about why we broke up. What if we got married and then a few years down the road he wants to break up? What if he remained closed off and eventually shut me out? What if we have kids by then? He had mentioned before we broke up that he was not sure he wanted children, but I thought that would change. That would be a deal breaker because I really wanted to be a mom. I loved children. I also thought if I accidentally got pregnant, he would accept it and we would be happy. I was trying hard to get past all the doubt because I really loved him and wanted my fairytale. I knew the doubts were hurting our relationship. I tried to push them out of my mind but they would not go away.

As a Christian, I know now that when you plan things without God's direction, it will not be right. Your life can never be complete unless you are His Child, follow Him and His call on your life.

Just before classes let out for the summer, Robert broke up with me for good. He said the truth was that he did not want to get married, to me or anyone. He said he had made the mistake of trusting someone who hurt him. He loved me but could not marry me. I tried to talk to him but he would not listen. He had already made up his mind. He was so sure of himself that it seemed as if he had been planning this for a while. I wondered if he had been planning it since the semester began when we came back from Christmas break. Things were definitely different after that. I did not feel like he was being completely honest about his reasons for ending our relationship. He would not talk to me. I was heartbroken. I thought I would never feel love like this, and I did not want to again if it just caused so much pain. I felt so vulnerable and a bit stupid for trusting this man with my heart. He was the love of my life. He was a senior and graduating. He left me standing in the parking lot of my dorm and walked away. I never saw him again.

Today as I think about my relationship with Robert, he was a bit closed off. He knew what he wanted in a relationship and did not consider me or my opinion. I think he was insecure because of the previous relationship. He had trouble seeing beyond that breakup. It was like all his future relationships would be measured against that one and never measure up. I wonder if he may have still been in love with the girl he had been engaged to.

I was definitely surprised that he asked me to marry him. I did have doubts but chose to ignore them. I believed Robert was the right man for me. I did not have much experience with dating. He was my first serious relationship.

Marriage was not really a goal of mine—not something I thought about much.

When I first met Robert, I was so attracted to him but I did not think about marriage with him. The example of marriage with my parents was not that great. My dad was in control, and my mom just agreed with everything. I did not want to be that person. I saw myself getting my degree and moving away on my own. I did not think I needed marriage to be happy. I was not a Christian then, so I did not know what I wanted. When you think you know best, you really don't if you are not trusting God.

I accepted there was no hope of any kind of reconciliation with Robert even though I was heartbroken and did not really understand why he left. I don't think I would have gone back to him if he wanted to resume our relationship. Robert represented heartbreak and broken trust. I doubt I would be able to trust him. I would always wonder when he might leave me again.

CHAPTER 3

# *Summer*

Summer began very sadly for me. I took a job at the library and tried to disappear. I did not want to see anyone. I just wanted to be left alone. It was going to be a long summer.

One of the girls I worked with asked if I was seeing anyone. She wanted to introduce me to a friend of her boyfriend. I was not interested. I told her about Robert. She said it was just one date. She thought I needed to get out and try to get over Robert. I did not think that was possible. Please don't tell me to just get over it—so insensitive. Robert was my first love. I would never get over him and seeing another guy would not help. I really just wanted to wallow and stay in this pit. It was my comfortable place, my protection from further pain and heartbreak.

She was very persistent, and I finally gave in. I was not the strong, independent woman I am today. The me today would have told her to get out of my face and leave me alone! Most of my friends today don't believe I was ever naive and shy. Life has a way of toughening you up. Being a teacher also really made me strong. I could write another book about those experiences!

We went on a double date. Keith was pleasant and very easy going. We had a great time. I was surprised how good I felt around him. I agreed to go out with him again. Keith was so different from

Robert. Robert was so serious but Keith was very laid back and just fun. He was very handsome and charming. I was still very hurt over my relationship with Robert. I knew I should not be dating, but I needed a diversion. I needed relief from this pain. It was temporary though. I had fun with Keith but when I got back home, my heart was still hurting for Robert.

Keith and I saw each other about three times a week. He loved picnics and we spent a lot of time outdoors. We went fishing many times. We went on several weekend camping trips. He was very adventurous and carefree. He was the opposite of Robert. Keith was just the diversion I needed. We had no expectations of each other. A summer of fun and no strings. I liked him and knew he liked me. I knew it was not a permanent relationship. I didn't want that—not for a long time and maybe never. As I think about it now, it was a dangerous relationship which could not have a good end. I was burying the pain of Robert with Keith. I was drawn to Keith's bad boy image. He did what he wanted, and I was along for the ride! It was so different and exhilarating.

Keith and I never talked about anything serious. We just enjoyed being together. I could sense he might be hiding something, but I did not care. I did not want to know. I just wanted a fun time with him and nothing serious. He did say that my friend had told him I had just come out of a bad break up. I told him I did not want to talk about that. He accepted that but then asked if I still wanted to get married someday. I told him I did not think I would ever get married. I wondered where he was going with that question.

My mom did not approve of my relationship with Keith. She thought it was too much. I had not told her about Robert but I believe she knew something. I think as mothers, we sense when something is wrong for our children. I also believe we have to be careful and let our kids make some decisions for themselves, even if those decisions might not turn out well. They have to learn by experience.

*He is Always Faithful*

The last time I saw Keith was the first week of August. It was right before the beginning of fall semester. We had a wonderful summer together. I did not see a future with him. When he took me home, we sat on the steps where Robert and I had sat several months before. I told him our relationship was over and I was ready to get back to school. He agreed and said he was not looking for a serious relationship. We both agreed. Summer was over as well as our time together.

I found out a few weeks after we broke up that Keith had been seeing two other girls during the time we were dating. We had never talked about being exclusive, but I was shocked. I just assumed I was the only girl he was dating. We spent a lot of time together and I wondered when he had time to date one other girl, much less two! He was definitely not a guy to bring home to meet the parents! I was thankful it was only a summer fling!

Keith called me several weeks after school started and wanted me to have dinner with him. I asked him about the other girls he had been seeing while we were together. He lied and said that was not true. He said he really liked me and wanted to keep seeing me. He said I was the one he wanted to be with, and he missed me. He did not want to break up but only agreed because he thought that is what I wanted. I agreed to see him but only because I wanted to confront him about his lies. I knew several people who knew these other girls and I could rely on their information. He came to pick me up and I met him in the parking lot of the dorm. I told him about what I knew. He was very angry, got in his car, and took off. I never spoke to him again.

That was guy number two that left, and I never saw again. I see a bad pattern here. I was definitely ready for a break from relationships. I decided to stop dating and concentrate on school. I wanted to get my degree and have a good life.

Today, I am aware of how the choices we make in life affect the rest of our lives. Those choices remain with us, and we must live with the consequences. I also know that God is the great healer and will make it right. He has done that for me. We cannot erase what has been done, but we can heal, move one, and live for Him.

God was still not a part of my life at this point. How did I survive for twenty years without Him? I believe in The Providence of God, which is the protective care of God. It can be explained as a preparation for the future. Even though I was not yet a Christian, God was preparing me for what was to come.

CHAPTER 4

# *Decisions*

Fall is my favorite time of year. The cooler weather is so relaxing. All the different colors of leaves are so pretty to see and admire. I went for many walks alone reflecting on the bad decisions I had made during the past year. I felt so different and not like myself. I did not feel right. I could not shake the feeling that something was wrong.

I had not been feeling well for a few months. In November, my friend's mom insisted I go to her doctor for a checkup. I liked the doctor right away. He was very pleasant and friendly. He told me I was pregnant. I was not surprised. I pretty much knew what was going on but was afraid to have it confirmed. I was four months with a late spring due date. I felt really alone. I was not sure what I would do. I lived in the dorm. My only job was work study on campus. How could I support myself and my child?

I decided not to tell Keith. I was afraid he might want to get married. One night back in the summer while we were still dating, we were sitting on his porch talking. He asked what I would do if I got pregnant. I told him I had never thought about it. He asked if I would marry him if I was pregnant. I was stunned. I knew I did not want to marry him.

I did not love him and would not get married just because I was pregnant. I just said maybe. I was not strong enough to stand up to him and say no. I knew he was not someone I wanted to be with forever. I thought something else was going on with him, but this is my story and not his. It was just something I sensed about him and his motives. When we have a close relationship with someone, we can sense things about them. I knew there were things going on with him, but he was not much of a talker. He told me his future wife would not be working. He said she should stay home and take care of the house and the kids. Is this the fifties? Is he kidding? Keith is definitely not the man for me. After my relationship with Robert, I definitely did not want to be serious with Keith or anyone else. I did not care to know anything of a serious or personal nature. This was another reason I decided not to tell Keith. I never considered that he might get upset when and if he found out I was pregnant. I was also afraid that I might not be able to stand up to him. Today I would have no problem talking to him.

One evening, several friends and I were walking to the local ice cream place. It was obvious I was pregnant. My friend Linda said she noticed a car was going very slow on the street and watching us. I glanced over and it was Keith. I told them to ignore him and just keep going. He saw us go into the ice cream shop. He could have easily parked and come inside, but he did not. He knew I was carrying his child but he did not care enough to do anything. I had no doubt that I had made the right decision in not telling him.

I was afraid to tell my parents. I did not tell them until I began to show. They pretty much had it figured out by that time. My dad said I would move back home, get a real job, and take care of my baby. He did not ask me what I wanted to do. In his mind, he was still in charge of me. He was very upset when I said I was not going to do that. He thought he could make me do what he wanted. He did not see how harmful that would be for both my baby and me. I did not tell them earlier because I knew how my dad would react, and I did not want that drama.

My dad was an alcoholic, and I did not want my child in that environment. My dad was a loving and caring man. He could also be angry and scary when drinking. My childhood was difficult, and I wanted better for my child. I remember one night, I overheard my parents talking. They were talking about me dating. My dad was telling my mom that he was concerned about me. He did not want me to end up pregnant like her. The next day I told my mom I had heard them talking. She explained that I was two when they got married and my dad was actually my stepdad. It was shocking, to say the least. I had not expected that news. This was another reason I did not date much in high school.

My family is Native American, Cherokee tribe. I never noticed until that day that my brothers and sisters were much darker than me. This was my family. This is a great example of how kids don't see color. If only adults could be like that.

My parents lived with my Grandma in a three bedroom house. I had three younger siblings still living at home. My brother slept on the couch and did not have a bedroom. It was a small house. There was no place where my baby and I would fit. Living with them was not an option. It was hard to be excited and happy with this life growing inside of me. I tried to be happy because I knew it affected my baby. It was a long, anxious nine months.

My mom was very supportive. As a mother of six, she knew the difficulty I faced.

Her life of trying to keep the peace in our family was not easy. She would agree with my dad when he was around, but secretly let me know she would support the decision I made regarding my baby. On my third doctor visit, the doctor asked what my plans were for my baby and me. I told him I was not sure. He knew I was a college student and living in the dorm. I told him about my dad and not wanting my child raised in that environment. He asked if I would ever consider adoption. I had not thought about that.

He said he had some close friends who were unable to have children. He said they were wanting to adopt. I told him I would think it over. He assured me again that they were a great couple who would love and support my baby. I wondered how someone who was not a biological parent could love a child as much as the biological parents.

Today, I am a retired teacher of forty plus years. I developed a close relationship with my students. There were many students I could have taken home and loved as my own.

I talked it over with my mom and friends. On my next visit, I told my doctor that I had decided on adoption. He assured me that my baby would be in a wonderful home, be well taken care of and loved. He was a great doctor, and I trusted him. It was also very sad to realize that I would not be keeping my baby—this baby who was connected to me and part of me. I would not be my baby's mother. I would never be a part of his or her life. Maybe, I would never see my baby. Could I really do this? My decision was made. I did not change my mind.

My dad was really angry at the thought of adoption. He said this was not just my baby, but that the baby belonged to our family. My baby was to be their first grandchild. Today, as a grandmother, I can understand that disappointment. I could not tell my dad why I chose adoption. He was a proud man and saw nothing wrong with his life. I don't think he ever understood my decision. After my child was born, he told the family we were not to talk about my baby again. I would have to go on with life as if my baby never existed. My baby would always exist in my heart. Did my dad really think I would or could just forget about my child?

My dad was also angry with me because he saw I was growing up and no longer under his authority. As a mother, I understand that today. When my son Zack drove away without me in his car for the first time, it did something to me that I cannot explain. As a mom, it's hard to see our children as adults. The first few times I sat in church and listened to Zack preach, I was in awe of the man he had become. He was grown up and sounded so mature and wise. It was a blessing for sure.

I want to insert a funny story here by asking a question. Do you remember when you were first attracted to someone? I remember coming home from school one day and telling my mom that I thought I was getting sick. I told her that I felt strange when I was around this boy in my class. I was short of breath and had trouble speaking. I was in the eighth grade. There was this boy whose name was also Robert—but not the Robert from the earlier part of my story. My mom laughed and told me I liked him. She also told me I was too young to have a boyfriend and to stay away from him! I remember it was the strangest feeling. I still remember how different I felt.

CHAPTER 5

# The Birth of my Child

May 3, 1974, my child was born. It was evening and very stormy, much like many spring days in Oklahoma. I still have sad feelings when it is stormy and rainy, remembering that day. You would think after forty years it would not affect me, but the feelings still remain. I do have peace now about my decision, but it is still painful. My baby needed a future I could not provide—a real family. I loved my child enough to want to give that to my baby. The feeling of the loss of my baby will be with me forever.

I really wanted to be with my friends when I went into labor. I was visiting my family for the weekend. I got up from dinner and my water broke. My parents took me to the hospital. I was distressed because I was at my parents' home. I did not plan for my dad to even be involved given his attitude. It would have been so much better if my family was not even involved. I was worried about my younger siblings as well. They did not need to be involved. I learned you can't really plan the birth of a baby!

The birth of my baby is a blur. The delivery room was very dark. I had a wet cloth over my face. It was actually really scary. I try to remember the events. It's difficult because I have tried to forget for so many years. I remember the pain of not seeing or touching my baby—the baby I carried for nine months. When I look at my grandchildren today, I could not imagine life without them, knowing they were alive but never knowing them or sharing in their lives. There would be no bonding. They quickly took my baby out of the room. They shared nothing about him or her with me. They did not tell me if my baby was a boy or girl. They never asked if I wanted to see my baby. They made that decision for me. There was no consideration for me or my feelings. The doctor never came back to see me after the delivery. He had my baby and did not really care about me. He was not the nice doctor I had trusted. I wanted to scream and felt like dying. There was one nurse who was very attentive and kind. I wondered if she had shared a similar experience. She seemed so compassionate. I could tell because she gave me extra attention. She would spend more time talking with me. I remember the next morning after I gave birth, I was reaching for my glasses as she came into my room. She mentioned that I reminded her of her daughter looking for her glasses as soon as she awoke. I wondered if she thought that I could be her daughter in a similar experience. I saw her a few years later at church. I realized her Christian heart was hurting for me. I saw Jesus in her, and that made an impact on my heart. She was very kind and talked to me a lot at church. She would ask how I was doing. She never mentioned my situation at church. I knew her mom heart was empathetic toward me.

I signed the adoption papers the next morning in my hospital room. It was a private, prearranged, closed adoption. Legally, I had no rights to the baby I had carried for nine months. I was left with despair, pain, and grief. It was hard to accept that my flesh and blood child would be gone, away from me forever. I was not a mother, and I would never be my baby's mother.

Adoption was very different in 1974. I was told nothing. It was pretty strange even back then to not know if my baby was a boy or girl. They could have at least told me that much. I was a naive, shy 19 year old. I did not ask any questions. I think I was afraid of the answers and was ashamed. I was in pain physically and emotionally and just wanted it to be over. I wonder if I was coerced. All these years later when I close my eyes, I still see the dark delivery room and the curve of my baby's back. I also wrestle with guilt that my child will be forever scarred because I was his mom and left him at the hospital. I know there is nothing I can do today, and that is hard to accept.

My mom told me a few months later that my dad asked to see the baby after the birth but they would not let him. He was very angry. He and my mom left and did not return to the hospital. They never checked on me or made sure I got back to my dorm. It was months before I even saw them again. It changed our relationship forever. We never talked about it again. My dad died many years later without ever discussing my baby. I wonder if he carried guilt and regret as well. I am a grandmother now and realize how painful that must have been for both of them. My baby was their first grandchild. I can understand how hard it is to have a grandchild that I might never see or be a part of their lives. I am blessed to have a close relationship with Zack's children.

I went home three days later. It was as if my baby did not exist. It's hard to remember the days, weeks, and months after leaving my baby at the hospital. They are all still a blur to me. I have a vision of myself curled up in a fetal position on my bed in my dorm room. I slept for days and it was hard to eat. I felt empty, just a shell of who I used to be. I did not want to face the world. I only went to class and back to the dorm, only doing what was necessary to survive but not really caring if I did. I really did not care if I lived. I did not feel like I could talk to anyone, no one would understand. My life changed forever because of that decision. I realized that this would never be over. I wanted to go where there was no pain but knew that place did not exist.

Years later, one of my closest friends from college, Regina, said she remembers that I told her and my other friends on our dorm floor that I did not want to talk about my baby ever again. She also told me she knew the sex of my baby but the person who told her made her promise not to tell. This person also knew where my baby was living. That would have been more information than I could handle. I was not yet a Christian. Today, I believe God protects us from things that He knows are too much for us. I am not sure if I would have looked for my baby, but I know I did not need that information. As a Christian, I know God reveals some things to us and keeps others to Himself.

> *Job 10: 11-12 You clothed me with skin and flesh, and wove me together with bones and tendons. You gave me life and faithful love, and your care has guarded my life.*

I remember feeling so lost and empty. I did not know God would use the birth of my baby to show me how much He loves me. After I became a Christian, I prayed for God's protection over my baby. Many nights I cried out to God for my child.

It was finals week, so I had to finish the semester. I can't remember much about that week. I did pass that semester with a c+ average. I decided to go to summer school. The summer of 1974 would be very different from the previous summer.

There was a young man in one of my summer classes who was interested in me. He asked me out several times. I told him no and to please leave me alone. I knew I did not want to be in a relationship for a long time, and maybe never. The lesson I learned was that relationships were nothing but trouble.

I went to summer school to keep busy and stay away from my parents. I think my dad realized that my Mom supported my decision and that made life very difficult for her. She was a strong woman who endured much at the hands of a husband who abused her emotionally and physically. She never complained and never said a negative word against him.

My mom died in 1978. She always wanted grandchildren but went to heaven without any. I am sure she felt the loss of my child almost as much as I did. There were several times that I sensed she wanted to talk to me about my baby but knew she could not go against my dad's orders. She would not deceive him and he would probably know if she was lying.

I prayed for thirteen years for my dad to be saved. I knew he needed Jesus. I hate the way he treated my mom and all the stuff he put her through. I recognized that it was the enemy who had control of his life. After my mom died, he had a really hard time for several years. He started drinking again. I rarely saw him during this time. He seemed closed off to the world. I prayed a lot for him. One day he called me, which was rare for him. He told me that two men he worked with had witnessed to him and prayed with him. He was saved that day. I could not stop crying. You pray for something for so long, you forget that it might actually happen!

My dad's birthday was coming up. I knew the perfect gift for him was a Bible. My dad is not a crier but he cried when I gave him the gift.

He had the Bible for many years. When it began to fall apart and look so ragged, I offered to get him a new one. He said no very emphatically. He said he did not need another Bible. This was to be his only Bible. It was all duct taped together and the cover was faded. My dad was not a talker. He did not talk much about personal things, but I knew he cherished that Bible. To him, it could not be replaced. I am not sure what happened to the Bible after he died, but I am sure it is still in our family.

> *Philippians 4:7 The peace of God, which surpasses all understanding, will guard your hearts and minds in Christ Jesus.*

## CHAPTER 6

# *I Met Jesus*

I had decided to never date or be in any kind of relationship again. It just brought pain and heartache. I was not interested in a relationship. I felt like I did not really deserve to be happy. I deserted and rejected my child. Why should a person like that be happy? I probably should have seen a counselor, but I did not. I was too ashamed and did not want to talk to a stranger.

A friend tried to persuade me to meet a friend of hers, but I was determined to not get involved with anyone for a long time and maybe not ever! I was done for a long time. I could not even think about seeing a guy because of the way my relationship with Robert and Keith had ended. I was not a Christian yet, and this is a good testimony of how we make terrible, heartbreaking mistakes without Jesus.

I met Sid in October of 1974. He was a Christian. He was also very handsome, charming, and persuasive. I told him I was not interested in dating. He was very insistent. I finally went out with him only because I was tired of resisting. I did like his attention and that he was so confident. There was something different about Sid. He was more concerned about me than himself. He was genuine, a word I could not use to describe Robert or Keith! Today, I know I saw Jesus in Sid. We saw each other several times and then decided we wanted to just see each other and not anyone else. It was a great relationship, but I got scared. I thought we were moving too fast. I did not want to tell him about my baby—did not want to go there with him. It had only been four months since I had my baby. I was still hurting. Breaking up with him seemed better than facing the truth. He was very upset. We did not see each other for over a month.

We eventually got back together. I realized I did love him and wanted to be with him. He asked me to marry him right before Christmas. I was ashamed to tell him about my baby. I knew I had to be honest if I wanted a relationship with this man. I also knew there was a strong chance he would walk away when he found out I was a mother and had turned my back on my child. I finally told him the truth. I really expected him to just walk away. He did not. He said that he already knew. There were people on campus that knew and had told him. He said he trusted me and was just waiting for me to tell him. It was amazing to see this man that loved me and saw real worth in me that I did not see in myself. I knew I had finally found the right man.

We got married during the summer. It was really wonderful. Sid took me to church. I accepted Christ at a revival a few months after we were married. I remember that day so clearly. I realized I was making my own decisions without regard to God. I had been going to church with a cousin the summer before I met Sid. I thought I knew what salvation was but realized I was doing things on my terms. I realized I had to repent, submit to Jesus as my Savior and let Him have control of my life. I accepted Him and knew he had and has a perfect plan for me. I know He loves me. As I write this, I have been a Christian for forty-four years. I can't remember not being a Christian and Jesus not being my Savior. I have a close, strong relationship with Him.

*Isaiah 12:2 Surely God is my salvation; I will trust and not be afraid. The Lord, the Lord Himself, is my strength and my defense; He has become my salvation.*

We were married for five years when I had my son Zack. I felt God was redeeming my life by letting me become a mother. It was really miraculous. We went to church as a family. I felt really happy with my life. We had planned to have another child when Zack was two but that was not part of God's plan for our lives.

The day Zack was born was so different than my first child. The delivery room was bright and cheerful. Sid was comforting, supporting and right by my side. The doctor and nurse were so helpful and caring. I did not feel alone. I knew there were people who cared about me and did not just want my baby. It was pretty amazing. Sid was a great dad. He was off two days during the week and would keep Zack while I worked so he did not have to stay with the sitter. It was so comforting to see him with Zack.

Sid and I had a good relationship for about seven years. We stopped communicating and our marriage fell apart after ten years. We divorced in May of 1985. It was heartbreaking, but I had seen it coming for a few years. We had stopped going to church. We had moved a few times with different jobs, and that is hard as well. When you stop relying on God and think you know what your life needs, it simply does not work.

Falling out of fellowship with God and His people is never a good decision. It reminds me of the story from the Bible of Jesus walking on the water and Peter wanting to join Jesus. As long as Peter kept his eyes on Jesus, he was fine. The minute he took his eyes off Jesus, he began to sink. My eyes had not been on Jesus for a while. We had also stopped talking and communicating, which is not good for a marriage. We grew apart and were no longer close. As I have already mentioned, I will not share many of the other details of this part of my story because it is not just my story. Others are involved and I want to be respectful of them and their families. I am hopeful that if they decide to share their story in the future, they will show me the same respect. I will always be grateful to Sid because he took me to church and I met Jesus because of him. We have a wonderful son in Zack as well. Our marriage did not last but God is still with me. He is sovereign and rules over all things with wisdom and His purpose will prevail.

It is unsettling to realize that just a year after I gave birth, I was married. It was just a short two years after my relationship ended with Robert and Keith. I should have given more thought to that decision. I can't help but think that this one decision has influenced every other decision I have made. I will never be whole until the relationship with my first child is reconciled. How will that ever happen? I think I was trying to fill the wound of losing my baby with another relationship. Today, I know only God can heal. He is our redeemer. I have no regrets regarding my marriage. God blessed me with Zack, Charlyanne and five wonderful grandkids. I trust God's plan.

> *Isaiah 46:10 I declare the end from the beginning, and from long ago what is not yet done, saying: my plan will take place, and I will do my will.*

Now I understand why I did not have more children. It is difficult to raise children as a single parent. God always provided for Zack and me, but at times, things were pretty tight. I was thankful to have a good job, a loving, extended family and church family. My school family was very supportive and helpful as well. God puts people in our lives who we need and who need us at exactly the right time.

Zack was saved and baptized when he was eight years old. We had a loving church family, which is so important when raising children who will love and follow God. I am so thankful to several men and women in our church who mentored Zack as he grew. I appreciate the men and women of our church who walked beside us and played a major part in Zack's life.

> *Jeremiah 31:3 I have loved you with an everlasting love; therefore, I have continued to extend faithful love to you.*

## CHAPTER 7

# *Where is My Child?*

I spent many years thinking about my first born child. When did he/she start walking, talking, and eating real food? Was he/she sick very much? How was the beginning of school? Each birthday was difficult, but I kept it inside. I did not share or talk with anyone about my feelings. I gave away my baby and signed away my parental rights. I had no right to even think about my baby. I had no right to even love my baby, but of course I did. I knew I might never see him/her. Loving my baby was all I might ever be able to have of my child. I loved my child and lifted him/her up in prayer every day. God was the only one I talked to about my child. He knew everything. He shed every tear with me. He is my Comforter.

*Psalm 119:50 My comfort in my suffering is this: Your promise preserves my life.*

During the early years of my child's life, I would see a family in a store and wonder if one of the children could be mine. Later on, I would wonder if one of the parents could be my child. I wondered if we had ever crossed paths. It is something that is difficult, but something that never leaves me. I always think about my child. Thoughts of my baby are always in the back of my mind. It was tough not knowing if my baby was a boy or girl. When I would meet someone new who was from the town where my baby was born, I wanted to ask their birthday and other personal information.

As a teacher, I would wonder each year about new students and parents I met. I would sometimes wonder if one of my students could be my child. In later years, I wondered if one of them could be my grandchild. I had no idea where my child was. Was he close or far away? Did he grow up in the small town where he was born, or did he and his family move away? I decided years ago that I would not look for him or her even though I thought about it most every day.

At family gatherings, I would feel someone was missing. My baby's birthday and Mother's Day were especially troublesome. I just wanted a small glimpse into my child's life.

> *Psalm 22:19 But you, Lord, do not be far from me.*
> *You are my strength; come quickly to me.*

I spent many nights praying about my child. One night, I could not sleep. I knew God could see how upset I was that night. I told Him I just really needed to know something about my child. I did not want to know his or her name. I just wanted to know if he or she was ok. Was my baby even alive? It was so troubling not knowing anything at all.

It was during this time of prayer that God revealed to me that my child was a boy.

God could feel my desperation while praying. He knew my deep desire to know something about my baby. From that day on, I knew my baby was a boy. I have a son. I felt relieved. It was the summer of 1994, and my son was twenty years old.

> *Job 11:7 "Can you search out the deep things of*
> *God? Can you find out the limits of the Almighty?*

*He is Always Faithful*

My son Zack was fifteen when I told him that he had a brother. I was concerned as to what his reaction would be. I told him I had to talk to our pastor about something important and then I needed to come home and talk to him. He said he would wait at home for me.

Our pastor told me he knew Zack was old enough and mature enough for my news. I was relieved to hear that. I knew Zack needed to know. There are people in my family who knew, and I did not want anyone else to tell him. I was also concerned that my oldest son might find me and show up on my doorstep. I thought that was highly unlikely, but it was a real possibility.

When I got home, I could tell Zack was anxious. I hoped that I had not scared him. He later told me that he thought I was going to tell him I was dying.

We both sat down. I told him I had to tell him something from my past that he needed to know. I asked him to just listen and when I was finished, I would answer any questions he might have. When I finished talking, he sat quietly for a long time. It was big news for a fifteen year old boy. I was a bit scared. He got up and came and stood by me and took my hand. He said, "You are my mom and I love you. There isn't anything you could tell me that would make me love you any less. Who am I, Mom, to judge you for anything you have ever done?" I was stunned. This from my fifteen year old son. God had his hand on Zack. This was the same summer that Zack was called into the ministry. We prayed together and I went to bed feeling so relaxed.

Zack and I had many conversations about his brother. He said it felt strange to know he had a sibling after being an only child for so long. He asked if he could tell someone. I said sure, but only a few. I asked them not to share. This is my personal story, and I was not ready to share. I was unsure when I would be ready. It wasn't that I was ashamed. It is a very personal part of my life and many people would be affected. I did not want to explain and answer a lot of questions. God would let me know when the time was right. Everything happens in His time, not ours. My trust is in Him.

> *Proverbs 16:9 A person's heart plans his way, but the Lord determines his steps.*

> *2 Peter 3: 8-9 But do not forget this one thing, dear friends: with the Lord a day is like a thousand years, and a thousand years are like a day. The Lord is not slow in keeping His promises as some understand slowness. Instead He is patient with you not wanting anyone to perish, but everyone to come to repentance.*

On May 3, 2014, my oldest son turned forty. I remember praying a lot that day and asking God if I would ever know anything about my son. Forty years is a long time, and I knew that a lot had happened in my son's life. I also knew God loved my son much more than I did. I trusted God to take care of my son. It is funny how a person who is essentially a stranger to me has impacted my life for forty years. 2014 was a hard year for me.

I considered buying a house. I prayed and checked into things, but it just was not the right time. I felt there were some big changes coming in my life. I had no idea what, but I knew God was preparing me.

Later that year, I was at a family reunion. Zack asked if I ever thought about my other child, and if I might have other grandchildren. I think about him almost every day. He is always here. Zack then told me that God had placed his brother on his heart to pray for him. Zack had been praying for him for the past three months without knowing why.

> *Psalm 145:9 The Lord is good to all, and His tender mercies are over all His works.*

CHAPTER 8

# *He would never call me mom*

On December 3, 2014, I received a message on Facebook asking for some very personal information. They wanted to know my maiden name, my age, where I was born and where I lived. They said they were looking for someone who would be about my age.

They asked, "Could this be you?" I read that message over and over in the midst of tears. I knew it was my son. I did not know what to do so I said no. They asked if I might know the person they were looking for. I said no. They said thank you and signed off. I sat and cried for the longest time. I knew it was him but I was scared and uncertain. I never expected to hear from him. I was not prepared to be contacted by him. It had been forty years. I had accepted that I would more than likely never know anything. I had decided that I would not look for him. I was concerned that his parents may not have told him he was adopted. I had placed him for adoption because I wanted a better life for him. If I found him and he did not know about his adoption, that would be very upsetting for him. I loved him and knew I never wanted to cause pain or heartache for him. I was also unsure how to look for him. I had no information except his date of birth and that I had a son. I did not have the money to hire a lawyer, so I thought it would be impossible to find my son.

I shared with Zack that someone was trying to contact me on Facebook. He said to just ignore them and not respond. He said not to communicate with someone I didn't know. I knew I could not ignore the message but was unsure what to do. I could not think about anything else and found it hard to concentrate. Several people asked me if something was wrong. I could not tell anyone so I just said I was fine.

A few days later, Zack called and asked if I had gotten any more messages from the person I had told him about. I said no, started crying, and could not speak for a while. He kept saying, "Mom, Mom." He then said, "You think it is him, don't you?" I knew it was him. That was a hard conversation.

Zack said I needed to respond. He wanted us to think about how to respond. He put himself in the situation right away. He is an incredible son. So supportive. Zack decided it was best if he talked to his brother first. We were unsure of my oldest son's intentions. Zack wanted to be sure it was safe. Zack asked me not to give any personal information yet. Zack was so quick to include himself in the situation. I was glad because there was no way I could do this alone. Zack's head was much clearer than mine!

Zack was five years old when I got divorced. I have not remarried. He and I have always been very close. It was just the two of us for so many years. I am so blessed to have him and his family in my life.

On December 12, 2014, Zack talked to my oldest son by way of text messaging most of the afternoon. His name is Doug. He is married with three children. Zack called later that evening saying, "Mom, it really is him. He is a family man and is fine. You can give him personal information. He really wants to hear from you." I will always remember that day. I was thrilled but nervous as well. I was still unsure of Doug and how he would react to me.

That was a Friday night. My weekend was out of control. I could not eat, sleep, or even think. I also could not stop crying. So much regret just flooded me. How could I leave my baby? How did I just walk away? I felt like I gave up on him. The day of his birth also came back: the dark delivery room, the abandonment by my parents, and the loss of my baby. Forty years seemed to be rushing at me from everywhere, flooding my soul with emotion. I thought I was losing my mind. It was overwhelming. I was afraid to even go anywhere because I could not stop crying. I was sure I looked crazy!

On Saturday afternoon, I called my friend Gladys. I told her I needed to talk. She let me come right over. I must have been at her house for over four hours. At one point, I tried to leave and she told me to sit back down, that I was not ready to leave just yet.

She is such an amazing Christian and the best encourager! I felt so much better after I talked to her. She is very positive. She told me it was good to have more family to love. I would never have looked at it that way.

I did not make it to church on Sunday. I was still such a mess. I knew I would fall apart if someone asked me how I was doing. I was not even sure if I should be driving.

I knew I needed to message Doug and that I was not going to settle down until I did. I messaged him at 5:20 on Sunday evening. It was very emotional. Doug was pretty emotional as well. I talked via Facebook messenger to his wife part of the time because he needed a break. I did feel better after messaging with Doug and his wife. I was able to sleep and make it to work the next day. We texted every day that week. I was still trying to comprehend that I was really communicating with my son. It felt like I had made a new friend that I was talking with and not my own son!

On Dec. 19, 2014, we spoke on the phone for the first time. We talked for over two hours, enough to run down both of our cell phone batteries! It was very easy and natural to talk to him. We both had questions about the same things. He just wanted to know that I was okay, and that is what I always wondered about him. As I sit at my computer today, I am trying to remember our first conversation. It was very good and reassuring. He played football in high school and said after he found out he was adopted, he would look in the stands and wonder if I was there, watching him. We talked about many other things, but I won't share much from that first talk as that needs to remain private out of respect for Doug and his family. It was reassuring to learn that Doug was doing well.

This past week brought me to a much deeper understanding of God—my loving, heavenly Father who loved me so much that He sent His only Son to the cross to die for my sins so I could live. I could live to know my own son and love him. He works everything in His time. I am truly content and complete in Him.

> *Psalm 33:4 For the Word of the Lord is right and true; He is faithful in all He does.*
>
> *James 1:17 Every good and perfect gift is from above, coming down from the Father of heavenly lights.*

God took every prayer I have ever prayed for Doug and put it together as only He can do. I have dreamed about meeting my son for so long. It is just amazing that it is really happening. I know that I deserve nothing, but God loves me so much that He let me know my son.

While I was waiting, God was working.

*Isaiah 40:31 says: Those who trust in the Lord will renew their strength; they will soar on wings like eagles; they will run and not become weary, they will walk and not faint.*

*Ephesians 3: 20-21 Now to Him who is able to do above and beyond all that we ask or think according to the power that works in us, to Him be glory in the church and in Christ Jesus to all generations, forever and ever. Amen.*

The above verses carry a lot of meaning for me. God planned it so I never have to wonder about my son again. I know where he is and that he is safe and happy. He grew up with a loving family. They raised him well. He was nurtured and loved. He has become a loving husband and father. I wondered how he felt when he found out he was adopted. Did he want to know me or know anything about me? He must have had questions. Did he ever wonder who I was or why I placed him for adoption? Did he ever feel rejected by me? I prayed that he was fine with being adopted. I knew he was from a loving home and prayed that was what he needed to accept being adopted. I did not raise him but he will always be a part of me. I love him.

This has me thinking back to when I was pregnant in college. This baby I was carrying who was a part of me was going to be another woman's child. I would probably never see him smile, hear his voice, or see him take that first step. He would never call me mom. He was physically and emotionally attached to me for nine months but now he would be forever detached from me. I walked away from the hospital without my baby and was no longer a mother. My baby was alone and not mine. I felt like a complete failure. I did not think my baby would ever forgive me. I did not deserve to be forgiven.

Ever since I found out about Doug, memories from 1974 come pouring out of me.

It is overwhelming, and some days I can't cope. I smell something, see something, or hear a song and a memory comes. I remember the emptiness, the ache in my stomach, the loneliness, wondering when I will be well again.

Today, I wonder how I squashed and hid all these emotions for so many years. I did not talk with many people—just too much explaining to do. I know God has carried me during this and many other tough times in my life. I have had days where the guilt is overwhelming. Guilt is so heavy. If you have carried something for so long, you know and understand the anxiety of it all. I can't take away anything that happened. I can start from here today and know that God washes me clean.

Forgiveness is difficult and ongoing for me. I know there are things I need to forgive and move on. I am working on it daily. When someone you love and care about hurts you, It is difficult to get over. It is compounded even more by the way things have not worked as I thought. I have let that go. I am still working through all these feelings and healing more each day.

I am realizing that I have never forgiven myself for placing my child for adoption. Writing my story revealed that and God is showing me how to forgive myself. I know I cannot change the past. I will start today, forgive, and be better by His grace and love.

CHAPTER 9

# *Reconciled with My Oldest Son*

I am just a few days from meeting my son, Doug. I keep looking at pictures of him and his family. I have not been able to think of much else since planning my trip to see them. My close teacher friend Angie said she did not see how I could be so calm. I am sure not calm on the inside! I don't want to bug people by talking about Doug and his family so much. I could do that all day! It seems like all I do is talk about him. My daughter-in-law Charlyanne said I do talk about him a lot but that is expected and people should understand.

It just does not seem possible that my son would want to know me, to love me and have me be a part of his family. When I look at his handsome face, I am amazed. This is really my son. The child I have prayed for, loved, and cried over all these years.

My prayer is that we would bond as a family and have a good time together. I have thought about Doug so much and for so long. Now I have a chance to be a part of his life and for him to be a part of my life. Lord, please bless and protect our time together.

I flew to North Carolina on March 13, 2015 for my first visit with Doug and his family. I had planned to stay just a few days because it was my first visit and I was unsure of how things would go. I was going to stay in a hotel, but they insisted I stay with them. They had a room all ready for me. They picked me up from the airport. It was almost an instant connection. I felt like I was with Zack and his family. We stopped for dinner, and by the time we got to the restaurant, I felt as if they had always been a part of me. It was like I was visiting them as I may have done many times before. It was so natural to talk with them. I was a part of their family. It was not awkward at all. I felt an instant sense of belonging.

The next day, we went on a day trip to Charleston, South Carolina. I had never been there. We spent the day shopping, eating, and sightseeing. It was fun to be together and get to know each other. The ocean was beautiful and so calming. I could have stayed there a while. We made plans to return again.

Doug is a fisherman. We spent Sunday at the lake. We fished and I caught a fish! I actually held the slimy thing in my hand. We were making some wonderful memories, ones I still cherish today.

I had planned to only stay a few days because it was my first visit. The night before I was to leave, I talked with them and decided to stay longer. I did not want to leave and did not think I could have left very easily. I extended my stay until Friday. Their boys had school, so it was a great time for Doug, his wife Leslie and I to spend time together during the day. One of the best days was when we went to Mount Airy, North Carolina, which is where The Andy Griffith Show was filmed. It is a sweet little town with lots of charm. One of my funniest memories happened when Doug asked one of the shop owners where Andy's house was located. She told us and said it is now a bed and breakfast. She then said when we go there, we can look but don't gawk! Just in case you don't know what gawk means: stare openly and stupidly, according to the dictionary! I was wondering how stupid I looked!

I came home on March 20th. My visit was more incredible and miraculous than I could have ever pictured in my mind. I was pretty sure we would get along well because we had texted and talked on the phone a lot during the past three months. It was still beyond anything I could have ever imagined. It was so much more than I could have ever dreamed. It was very natural and easy to be with them.

When they took me to the airport, Doug asked If I was happy. I told him I was very happy and felt complete now. I was a bit sad because I knew I would miss them, but we had already planned a summer visit.

May 3, 2015, was the first time I could call my son and say, 'Happy Birthday!' This birthday was joyful and not like the past years. I wrote the following poem and put it in a card I mailed to Doug:

### *Just Because*

*Just because it was my choice,*
*Doesn't mean I never wanted to hear your voice.*
*Just because I knew it was right,*
*Doesn't mean I did not cry every night.*
*Just because I walked away,*
*Doesn't mean I did not think about you everyday.*
*Just because I wasn't there,*
*Doesn't mean I did not care.*
*Just because I love you with all my heart,*
*I knew you would be better if we were apart.*
*Now our family is real,*
*My heart will heal.*
*Because God loves us all so much.*

I could never really put into words what this birthday meant but hoped this poem conveyed my feelings to him in a way he would understand.

During July of 2015, I made a summer visit and stayed for a month. The condo in which they live is beautiful. It is right on Lake Norman, which is breathtaking. I had my own room and woke up every morning looking out at the lake. I could sit outside, have quiet time, read, and pray. I took many walks by the lake. It was so peaceful. I really felt so content and at home. I had been praying and thinking about moving to North Carolina. I made the decision for sure on this summer visit. I was content and knew my decision was God's will.

The month flew by. We did not take any trips, but we spent a lot of time together. This was needed so we could get to know each other. We talked a lot, and I felt we really bonded as a family. We planned and cooked meals together—things a real family does. Spending time with them and getting to know them was what we all needed. We had several personal talks and shared personal things. I shared some things with them that I had not shared with anyone before that day. I felt comfortable sharing and being myself.

We did some furniture shopping for my move. We looked at different apartments and condos for me. It was really exciting and I was anxious for this new phase of my life. I was thankful to God every day for letting me be a part of this wonderful family.

Zack and his family were vacationing in Pigeon Forge, which is about three hours from where Doug lived. We made arrangements to meet in Pigeon Forge and spend the day and evening with Zack and family. This was the first meeting of our families. It was just wonderful. The kids got along and played. We went swimming and sat around just as a family does. We were all a family.

The rest of the month passed quickly. The day I flew back to Oklahoma was really tough. Doug and his boys walked me to the security area of the airport. I could not stop crying. Doug reached in his pocket and gave me his high school class ring. He wanted me to have something of his to keep. That was a special moment for me. I take the ring out every now and then to remember that moment.

In December of 2015, I flew to North Carolina and spent ten days during this visit. This was our first Christmas together as a family. We went to Charleston and spent three days on the beach. It was beautiful there. We swam in the ocean and sat in the sun and relaxed. It was hard to believe it was Christmas because the high temperature was eighty two degrees every day that we were there. It was just so natural being there with Doug and his family. God did much more than I could have ever thought possible.

I learned some important things when I was with them. They lived just a few miles from me in Oklahoma for several years. It is possible we crossed paths. Their oldest son was born at a local hospital which is about fifteen minutes from my house. I was stunned at some other things I learned. They told me that the doctor who delivered Doug told his parents I had changed my mind and was keeping Doug. He called Doug's parents the day after Doug was born and asked them if they still wanted a baby. I was very distressed to learn that my baby was truly alone for a while. His parents were not at the hospital waiting for him. I still struggle with that guilt. Hopefully, there were some wonderful nurses who cared for Doug. It also made me wonder if that doctor was up to something. I never paid for any doctor visits or the hospital stay. I don't remember asking about this or if the doctor told me anything about payment. I just assumed the adoptive parents had paid the bill. They could not have done so if they did not even know they were getting my baby. I wonder if the doctor might have considered adopting my baby himself. There are several unanswered questions remaining regarding the situation. If I could afford a private investigator, I might find out what happened. It is not that important to me at this point, but it would be interesting to know the truth.

When I found out that Doug's parents did not get him right after he was born, I had to be alone for a while. It was more difficult because I was not at home. I liked being in North Carolina with Doug and his family but I wanted to be home after hearing this news. I needed to be where I felt safe. I prayed earnestly for God to take this information and process it because it was just too much for me. I prayed that Doug would know I never rejected him. I loved him but saw no way to keep him. I prayed for God to give Doug an understanding heart and be accepting of my decision.

It was even more difficult to return home this time. I just wanted to be with them all the time. I really was a part of their family. It was just beautiful to be with them.

Have you ever thought about what it means to make up for lost time? Doug mentioned that a lot on my visits. I looked up the meaning. It means to compensate for something you have not done before. I don't think you can make up for lost time. I think you just need to make the best of the time you have together.

Forty years is a long time to wait to meet my son. I get to love him and call him my son. God's timing is perfect.

CHAPTER 10

# *The Big Move!*

I moved to North Carolina on September 14, 2016. Zack and my nephew Eric traveled with me. We rented a huge moving truck. My nieces and their families came to help pack up the truck and spend time with me before we got on the road. My sweet baby sister passed away the year before and my moving was a pretty emotional goodbye for all of us.

The trip was very pleasant. Zack drove the truck and Eric drove my car. I took turns riding with them. We got to Tennessee and had tire trouble. We planned to get to Pigeon Forge and spend some time there. We ended up waiting hours to get a new tire and got to Pigeon Forge after midnight. We were tired and went to bed.

The next day, we traveled through the Smoky Mountains. I had not been through that part of the country except for a short visit to see Zack and family at Pigeon Forge the summer before when I was visiting Doug and his family. I was just in awe of the mountains. It was beautiful. I could see the beauty and majesty of God. How could you look at those beautiful mountains and not believe and want to know God?

We arrived in Mooresville, NC about 3:30 on Saturday afternoon. Doug and his family were waiting for us. I had already rented an apartment. It did not take long to unpack the truck. We went to dinner and then just hung out together for a while. It was great to be with my sons, Eric included. He is more like a son than a nephew to me.

Zack prayed with me that night before we went to bed. It was wonderful to have my son pray over me. He told me that if I was not happy and wanted to come home at any time, he would come and get me. He also told me to try and stay at least a year!

My plans were to stay from three to five years at the most. I wanted to stay long enough to strengthen the bond with my North Carolina family. Oklahoma is my home. I knew that I wanted to be back home at some point.

Zack and Eric flew back to Oklahoma early the next morning. I was not prepared for the flood of emotions as I hugged them and dropped them off at the airport. I was going to be over a thousand miles away from them both, it was pretty heart wrenching. I had to go home and just chill out the rest of that day. Zack lived in Texas and was never more than a few hours away. Eric was only 20 minutes away from my home.

The first few months, I saw Doug and his family several times a week. I would pick the boys up from school a few days during the week, get them a snack, and take them home. There were days they stayed at my house until their mom picked them up after she got off work. I helped them with homework, just like a grandma does. They only lived a few miles away and school was close to my home. The boys would spend the night with me on Friday nights if I was not busy. I spent lots of time with the whole family, going to lunch or dinner, shopping and just hanging out at the pool. I was able to attend most of the boys' football games, which was incredible. I was getting settled.

North Carolina was feeling very much like home already. We spent our first Thanksgiving together. I had them over to my home for Christmas. It was really pretty wonderful.

I decided I wanted to substitute teach. I really missed being in the classroom. I went to a training class with the local school district and got plugged in to the schools in my area. I began subbing about three days a week. I could have worked every day but I wanted some free time. I liked getting to know the kids and teachers there. It felt really good to be part of the school community again.

I visited several churches before I found the one where I knew God wanted me to serve. I felt at home the minute I sat down. The children's minister, Katrina, was from Oklahoma and was so glad to see another Okie! There was a sweet couple who sat in front of me. They were so friendly and invited me to lunch after the service. I met another lady named Helen who became so dear to my heart. She invited me to ride with her to the restaurant. I felt like I was with family which I was, my church family.

They invited me to dinner the following Friday night. I met so many people that night. I joined Peninsula Baptist Church the following Sunday. It was good to be so connected already. God gave me these people to love and who loved me. Church is a big part of my life. I was blessed to have found my church home so quickly. As time went on, I was so grateful to have this amazing group of God's People. I saw how God was working by placing me at Peninsula Baptist Church in Mooresville, North Carolina.

\* \* \* \* \* \* \*

My relationship with Doug and his family began to change after Christmas. I did not see Doug and his family much at all during January and February. I had been texting with them daily and talking on the phone with them about two or three times a week. I saw them often. It seemed like it changed overnight. It just went to nothing.

When the first of March came around, I texted them and asked if something was wrong as I had not heard from them much. They said things were fine and they were just busy. That made sense as they had two sons who were very involved in sports. I had been picking up the boys after school several days a week. They decided on a different place for the boys without any explanation. I did not see them after this change. The boys did not spend the night anymore. I felt like the whole family was pulling away and distancing themselves from me. Doug had told me before I moved that he was excited that I was going to be a grandma to his boys and they would need help with the boys. That did not seem possible now that I was not seeing them on a regular basis or spending time with them. I prayed and God assured me that things were fine and I had no reason to be concerned.

Over the next few months things did not change. I rarely saw them or heard from them. I asked them again several times if I had done something wrong. I thought maybe I had offended them in some way. They assured me again that things were fine and they were just busy.

Things at church were going very well. I saw my group regularly at church and other events. We have a great group of senior adults who planned regular outings. We went to several places in the area. I was happy to see them and learn more about my community.

I really wished that I could have shared some of these places with Doug and his family. I was unsure what to do concerning them. The communication was pretty much nonexistent. I saw Doug some but not the rest of the family. I did not like seeing just him. I wanted to form relationships with the whole family and not just him. They did not seem to want to talk to me and continued to say things were fine. They were definitely not fine for me. I wondered if I had tried too hard. Did it become too much for them? I wondered what I had done wrong. Did they just decide having a relationship with me was not worth their time? I was upset and heartbroken that things did not seem to be working out as I had hoped or how I saw them working. I also came to realize that I did not really know them as well as I first thought. I had known them for two years before I moved to North Carolina. Before I moved, I had only seen the best parts of them, not the everyday life. This must be how they saw me as well. I think there were unrealistic expectations for them and for me as well. We definitely should have had a sit down talk about how we perceived things would work. I learned that they are really private and not the kind to talk about things. I am just the opposite. My life is an open book, so to speak.

I believe problems or misunderstandings need to be discussed and solved. I still had a lot of unanswered questions regarding the whole situation. I have felt guilt over this as well. I kept wondering what I did wrong and why they would not talk to me. Did they just not care to make things work? They seemed to shut me out of their lives without any explanation.

Zack suggested I plan a trip to Oklahoma for a visit. He thought that might help me see things more clearly. I was hoping it was not really as bad as I thought. I came for a visit to Oklahoma in April of 2017.

I stayed with a dear sister in Christ, Erma Lee. She was a gracious hostess. It was a true blessing to be with her. We spent many evenings talking. I gained great perspective from her about the issues I was facing. It was good to talk with someone outside of my situation who could give clear perspective and Godly advice as well. I really needed that.

> ***Proverbs 19:20*** *Listen to advice and accept discipline, and at the end you will be counted among the wise.*

I spent time with family and friends that week. It was great to be back in my home church and to be with my church family. During this visit, I pretty much made up my mind to move back to

Oklahoma, my true home. It was hard to get back on the plane, I just wanted to stay where I knew I was loved, wanted, and accepted.

Doug picked me up from the airport. Things were definitely strained. He felt like a stranger. It was a quiet ride home. I was not sure how to tell him I was moving back to Oklahoma. He must have sensed something because he asked if I was thinking about moving. I told him yes, I was planning to move. He was really quiet after that, what could he say, really? When I dropped him off at his house, he said he was fine with me moving. He did really seem like he was fine. I thought that was going to be a hard conversation. It did bother me that he did not seem concerned with my decision. I thought he might be a bit upset. His reaction told me a lot. It was a painful reaction for me.

I had a good talk with Doug a few weeks later. We talked about my move. I told him I was disappointed that things had not worked out for me in North Carolina. I made sure he understood that I was not blaming him and was not disappointed in him or his family. I was disappointed that things were not working. He said he knew things were not going well but was unsure as to what to do. I told him I felt the same way and was not sure if there was anything to be done. You can't force relationships. I think that when I finally met him, I thought everything would be perfect and we would have all the answers. I thought we would just mesh and be a family. We actually did not know each other that well and still do not today. Maybe we were just too different for it to work. I have learned that they were who they were long before I met them, as was I. I learned that my values and beliefs were different from Doug and his family's. They were strangers—ironic when you think about it. I gave my baby to strangers and now he is a stranger to me. Those are things I had not thought about in making my decision to move to North Carolina.

We have no history. A reunion does not make us a family. The love and trust of a family takes time. I think I tried to rush the whole process. Forty years of nothing, and then everything all at once. New relationships take time. I may have offended them because I was getting too close. They are a tight knit family and perhaps there was no room for me. I came to realize that family is not only blood relatives but people who love and support you.

I will never know the feeling of someone who finds out they are adopted. How does it feel when you find out the parents you loved and who loved you were not your biological parents? How could your mother who carried you for nine months, was part of you, shared only things a child and mother can share, give you to strangers? I wonder if there is something missing even if you had a wonderful childhood and amazing parents? It would be hard to accept for sure. I may just be trying too hard to understand. Some answers may be only for God.

I had to step out on faith and trust God with making the decision to move to North Carolina. I prayed and had peace from God. Others prayed as well and were very supportive. I will not stop trusting because it has not worked out the way I wanted. The Bible does not promise that we won't encounter trials. His word promises He will be with us. I know God has a plan. I trust Him. We must be willing to follow Him even though it may not be where we planned to go.

> *Isaiah 55: 8-9 For My thoughts are not your thoughts, nor are you ways My ways, says the Lord. For as the heavens are higher than the earth, so are My ways higher than your ways, and My thoughts than your thoughts.*

The story of Joseph in Genesis 37-44 in the Bible is one where we see Joseph trusting and following God even though things were difficult for Joseph. Joseph was his dad's favorite, which did not help him with his brothers. I am sure Joseph did not think his brothers would throw him in a pit and then sell him as a slave. They had actually planned to kill him but one of the brothers stepped in and they threw Joseph in the pit instead. The brothers then lied to their father about what happened to Joseph. Joseph went to Egypt without anything and was soon in charge of Potiphar's household. The Bible says Potiphar did not concern himself with anything with Joseph in charge. He was wrongly accused by Potipher's wife and ended up in prison. In no time, He was granted favor with the prison warden. Joseph was put in authority over all the other prisoners. The Bible says the prison warden did not worry about anything with Joseph in charge. It also says that God was with Joseph and he was successful even in the midst of his situation. Potipher and the prison warden saw God in Joseph. Joseph trusted God in the midst of all his troubles. He did not waiver.

> *Proverbs 3; 5-6 Trust God from the bottom of your heart; don't try to figure out everything on your own. Listen for God's Voice in everything you do, everywhere you go. He's the One who will keep you on track.*
>
> *Psalm 139:16 All the days ordained for me were written in your book before one of them came to be.*

These verses don't say to just trust God during the good times. He is there in every circumstance, good or bad, of our lives. We need to trust Him, not ourselves.

CHAPTER 11

# *A Strange Summer*

The summer of 2017 was quiet, peaceful and extremely lonely at times. As a teacher, summer was always my time to recoup, rest, and enjoy vacations! This year was very different. I tried to plan some things with Doug and his family, but they weren't receptive. They did not seem interested in seeing me or spending time with me. I could feel Doug and his family pulling away. This was something I feared in the beginning when I first met them but had not thought about in a while.

I began to think Doug might not really be fine with my decision to move. He might also be pulling away from a situation that was not meant to be. I wondered if Doug was not accepting of my boundaries.

I began to experience lots of regret. Was that a normal part of my situation? I know I made an inconceivable decision by placing my son with a family who needed him. They loved him and raised him well. I wanted him to have a much better life than I could offer, and that happened for him. Still, I wonder how it would have been if I would have kept my son? Would we have even had a chance? It seems I keep reliving all that shame, hurt, and guilt all over again.

I don't remember feeling much after I came home from the hospital alone. Now I am feeling a lot of regret, pain, and grief. I am having a hard time dealing with all of it. I don't think I ever grieved the loss of my baby. I must have kept it all hidden, thinking it would just go away if I tried to forget. I realized I needed time to grieve. God will help me through all of it.

> ***Isaiah 41:10*** *So do not fear, for I am with you; do not be dismayed, for I am your God. I will strengthen you and help you; I will uphold you with my righteous right hand.*

Doug and his wife had given me a copy of the adoption papers. I still cry when I read those papers. The words termination of legal rights cut right through me. Hurt and rejection set in. I have no legal rights to my son. I am not his mother, except for my physical role in carrying him for nine months. I placed him with strangers. He would be forever known by their last name and not mine. My name would not be on his birth certificate. If you are a parent, think about that for a minute. There are no words to describe how that makes me feel. It was as if he was never mine or a part of me. Why should I even have any rights? It was like he died but he is alive and not mine. There are just no words for the feeling of that loss. There is no feeling to describe the loss and grief over someone who is still alive. I thought we would always be linked—that he would always be a part of me. The truth is we were disconnected the moment they took him from me in the delivery room. I can't get that back. It is gone. Even today, there are days I still relive that grief.

I was asked by several friends if I was resentful toward Doug's parents because they became his parents and not me. I am not at all. I am nothing but thankful for his parents. They took Doug in, loved him and gave him a home, which I could not do. It is unsettling to me that they knew about me but I never knew anything about them. The adoption papers have my name on them and Doug's parents as well. I am sure the reason I signed the papers in my hospital room and not in court is so I would not see their names on the documents.

God knows the whole situation and He knows my heart. He has a plan and is already there. He is always with me. I am never alone. Hope is found in Him alone. Help me Father, to trust you in all things.

* * * * * * *

By the end of June, I was ready to be home. I checked to see what it would cost to go ahead and move. It was very expensive to get out of my lease and move home. It would have pretty much drained my savings, and I knew I should not do that. I prayed and God brought me comfort. It would be a long time until September. I tried again to plan a few things with them, but it just never worked out. I began to realize that I would not see Doug and his family much if at all. I saw this as a resting time with my Heavenly Father. I studied scripture a bunch. It was definitely a learning time as well.

Spending time at the pool was helpful and relaxing. It gave me lots of time to think. There were usually only a few others at the pool, so it was nice and quiet. I definitely needed that relaxing time.

My church family was so supportive during this time. I was very close to several of them and confided in them. They often took me to lunch or dinner. I spent time at some of their homes. It helped to have private talks with them. I helped out with our church's children's camp. It is good to help others when we are in a difficult situation.

We see the blessings of God in others' lives in amazing ways. It is great to be with other believers and share that love.

> *Matthew 7: 24-25 Everyone who hears these words of mine and acts on them will be like a wise man who built his house on the rock. The rain fell, the*

*rivers rose, and the winds blew and pounded the house. Yet it did not collapse, because its foundation was built on the rock.*

These words from Matthew 7 have brought me so much comfort and peace. I am a Child of the King. My house is built on the Rock who is Jesus. I rest in the fact that God loves me and will always be here with me.

I have unanswered questions. I may never know what happened or what went wrong. I am trying to accept that I will not be part of their family. I have not seen much of them at all this summer. I can't build a relationship with people I don't spend time with or hardly see. I think I was thinking too much with my heart and not my head. I was so caught up in the fairy tale of everything and was not thinking clearly. God will help me accept whatever happens. I know moving to North Carolina was part of His plan. I do have answers regarding my oldest son. I will learn to accept whatever happens. I have learned a lot about myself through this experience. I know that only by God's grace will I find the strength I need. God is making everything right.

My final trip before moving was with my church friends to Boone, NC. It was so peaceful to be in the mountains. God's beauty and majesty are so real there. We went to Grandfather Mountain and walked across the mile high bridge. I am a bit afraid of heights, but I had no trouble crossing the bridge. I felt like I really accomplished something. I know it helped that my friends/church family were there with me. Their love and support mean so much even now. I am still close to them. They will always be my North Carolina church family.

\* \* \* \* \* \* \*

I wrote this poem a month before I moved. That evening I was feeling like I did when I left Doug at the hospital and came home alone. Some days I still feel really wounded. I cry out to God, and He brings me healing and peace. His grace is everlasting.

### Love Just Hurts

*You give your heart away,*
*Knowing it is all you can do.*
*You pray for this child you love,*
*Years go by, still you pray and love.*
*Your mind gets settled,*
*Your heart won't let go.*

*Then hope comes,*
*You hear from this child you love.*
*Life is good for a while,*
*Then things get quiet.*
*Not much word from this child you love.*
*Still you pray and hope.*
*Finally you know you must move on,*
*You must let go of something*
*You never really had. So you pray,*
*God brings peace.*

*Sometimes love is good,*
*Sometimes love just hurts.*

**Lamentations 3:25** *The Lord is good to those whose hope is in Him.*

I believe that God has a purpose for every tear, every pain, and every heartache. Nothing happens by accident. He is sovereign. He has absolute control of all things. He can bring good out of all things. I may not see the good, but I trust Him. He is making me more like Jesus.

> *Jeremiah 29:11 "For I know the plans I have for you," declares the Lord, " plans to prosper you and not to harm you, plans to give you hope and a future."*

In her book, <u>He Can Be Trusted,</u> Melody Box writes: "God's vision is perfect and far-seeing while ours is dim and distorted, and near-sighted. We only see the pain, the fear, the sadness, the ugliness, the evil, the loneliness. We see the current, the right now. God sees the comprehensive view, from beginning to end. He sees our complete story, and we can trust that the end of our story will be better than all the other chapters!"

God will use our disappointing, heartbreaking times for good. We don't see this when we are in the middle of all the pain. We just want the pain gone and our lives back to the normal we remember before all the madness. When you have longed for and dreamed about something for so long and then it does not work out as you planned, it is really hard to pick yourself up and keep going. God picks us up in a way only He can do.

Melody also says: "God loves you whether you believe it or not. He loves you whether you think you are worthy of His love, whether you are angry with Him because of the darkness you are living in, or whether you even doubt His existence. He loves you and accepts you exactly as you are right now. And there is nothing more I can add to that." Melody has written a great book, one I highly recommend. I have gifted several copies to friends dealing with great disappointments and it has impacted them as well.

After things hit bottom for me, I had several people wonder why I was not mad at God. Didn't He give me something and then take it away? I realize that the choices we make have consequences. It was my choice, and it was not God who took my son away. God loves us in spite of those choices. He is my anchor, and He is my hope when I am drowning. If I did not cling to and be held by Him, I would have drowned. At the end of the day, He is and always will be here.

*2 Timothy 4:17 But the Lord stood with me and strengthened me.*

## CHAPTER 12

# *Back To Oklahoma*

I woke up during the first week of September feeling so grateful for my year in North Carolina. I could focus on the negative. I could just pull the covers over my head and refuse to face the day. There have been days I have wanted to do just that! I choose joy because I am a child of the King. I met some wonderful people in North Carolina. I was able to spend time with my oldest son who I did not even know a few years ago. God is leading me home to Oklahoma, and I am excited for new opportunities.

I moved back to Oklahoma on Sept.15, 2017. Zack, Eric and his wife Sarah all flew into Charlotte to take me home. I talked to Eric several times, and he seemed excited. He kept saying they were coming to get me and bring me home!

It was a three day trip. When you are driving a moving truck full of stuff, you cannot drive very fast through the mountains. It was great riding with Zack. I was able to talk through a lot of stuff with him. He is a good listener and great counselor. God has blessed me so wonderfully with him and his family. I was so thankful to Zack's wife Charly for being so gracious with sharing Zack's time so he could make the trip again just a year later. She remained in Texas with their four kids. Zack and Charlyanne have both helped me tremendously through this difficult time. I appreciate Charly so much because she is honest with me. She does not just tell me what I want to hear, and I appreciate that. I understood things much better because of that. I am so glad God brought her to my son. She is an amazing wife and mother to my grandkids.

I received a call from my former principal Alison a few weeks after I was home asking if I would sub for a former teammate, Nicole, for the following week. I was glad because I really needed to be busy. When I arrived at school, my principal told me that my teammate had decided to stay home with her baby. She also told me the job was mine if I wanted it. I was thrilled. I love teaching and being back at my home school was a blessing. It was second grade, and with two of my favorite teacher teammates, Angie and Amber! It was going to be a fun year! It feels so good to be back in the groove!

This job was something I really needed. God knew that. He meets our very need. He put me back in my school from which I retired just a year earlier. I knew most of the teachers and staff. Several people who I saw in the hallway during the day would tell me how glad they were that I was back. They said I was really needed at Freedom. I never voiced it, but I needed them just as much, if not more than they needed me. I felt so secure with being a part of my school family again. My close teacher friend Suzanne has such a great listening ear and good insight. It was good to be just down the hall from her as well. I was definitely glad to be back at Freedom. It was good to feel their love and support.

There were so many days I just wanted to stay in bed and not face the world. I could almost feel God's gentle nudge to get me up and going. There were days I wanted to scream, 'Just leave me be.' He loves us too much to leave us where we are. He gave me this job because He knows best and He knew where I was needed. Helping others aids in our healing as well.

I had a small class of nineteen second graders. We really connected after just a few days. These kids were mine. I loved them and they loved me. We had great days together. It was a beautiful school year. I still go back to my school and sub teach.

When I see those kids, it just touches my heart. They come and hug me and seem to never let go. God is good all the time. In the midst of my heartache, He gave me these children to love and teach. I am amazed at how He puts everything together at exactly the right time. He always knows what we need.

\* \* \* \* \* \* \*

Things really broke down with Doug and his family after I was back in Oklahoma. I did not hear much from Doug and his family at all. The last phone conversation I had with Doug was October of 2017. He asked if I was getting all moved in and settled. I said yes. He asked if it was good to be back in Oklahoma. I said yes. He then told me that I should have never moved to North Carolina. He said he did not understand why I had even moved to North Carolina. He said if it were him, he would have never left Oklahoma. I was stunned and could not even speak for a few minutes. I then had to hang up because I just could not talk to him anymore. It was really more than I could comprehend. I just kept playing the conversation over and over. Did he really say those things? What did he mean? Why would he be so hurtful? Did he really even think about what he had said? The more I thought about it, the angrier I became. Did the past few years mean nothing? I gave up my life here in Oklahoma to be with him and his family, to make a life with them. I felt like I had sacrificed a lot to make this move. I even retired early to make the move. It seemed like it was all for nothing. It was like it did not mean anything to him. Did he just really not care? I wondered if that was why they stopped seeing me when I still lived there. I wanted to call him back and really let him have it, but I did not. If my actions meant nothing, then my words would be worthless as well.

Doug, his family and I had talked a lot about my move over the past two years. They were always positive, excited and said they could not wait for me to be close to them. Doug told me he was happy that I would be in their lives and never be apart from them. What could have happened for them to make such a drastic change towards me?

Why weren't they comfortable talking to me about a problem they may have had with me? Maybe I should have titled this book: unanswered questions!

I waited a week and tried to call Doug. He did not answer and did not return the phone call. I texted him several times but no response there. I did not hear from his wife either. They became totally silent. I want to be mad and bitter but know that will only hurt myself. I asked Zack if he had heard from Doug but he had not. It was strange.

I did not hear from Doug for the rest of 2017. I tried to text him on New Year's Day of 2018 but did not get a response. It was puzzling that I would hear nothing from him. I would have appreciated a reply and explanation. I decided to stop calling and texting because he did not return phone calls or texts. I am left wondering what went wrong. They shut me out completely and I don't know why. They did not respect me enough to be open and honest.

There were many sad and depressing days ahead. The rest of 2017 and part of 2018 were some of the most dismal days I have experienced in my life. I did not know I could cry as much as I did. I went to bed by 8:30 most nights because I was exhausted and needed to block it all out. It seemed my world had fallen apart, every dream I had regarding Doug and his family had gone down the drain. I felt like I was paying for all the foolish, sinful choices I had made in my life. At times like this, I feel like that shy, vulnerable young mother again. My Comforter was right there with me every day. I am grateful for the loving family and friends who helped me more than they realized. I would not be where I am today without their love and support. Thanks so much friends for your grace!

I texted Doug on his birthday in May but got no response. I did not hear from Doug until June of 2018. I told him I was making a visit to North Carolina in a few weeks. He responded and asked me to text him when I arrived. I texted him and his response was that he did not realize I was coming to visit so soon. I did not understand his response. I had just told him two weeks before when I was arriving. I was there ten days but I never saw him or his family. I never heard from him again while I was in North Carolina. I was not sure about seeing them either but I was hoping to try and see if we could meet for lunch or dinner. It may have been awkward but I wanted to try. Maybe I was just hoping for too much, too soon. It was disappointing. I was hoping Doug could be honest and just say he was not ready to see me. I would have been sad, but I would have understood. It would have been better than silence.

I am so grateful to Susan and the rest of my church family at Peninsula Baptist Church in North Carolina. Susan opened her home to me and we had the best time. We visited several places in Charlotte, Davidson, and Morrisville, NC. It was great to be with her and see familiar places. We went on a boat tour of Lake Norman. Susan is a great listener as well. I was able to spend time with my Sunday School group and other friends. It was great to be with them again.

At this time, I do not have any plans to return to North Carolina. It was really painful to know that Doug and his family were so close and I was no longer a part of their family. I realized that I may never have been a part of them. The instant happy reunion was not real. Understanding that was part of the problem. I learned a reunion does not guarantee we will be a family or that I will be part of that family. I have good memories of North Carolina, but the disappointment of everything is just too much for now.

The last morning during my visit in North Carolina had me thinking of my journey the past few years. I was so happy to meet my son. I just knew life would be perfect after I met them. I felt like I would never have any need for anything again. I felt whole again. I am sure some of you can relate. I learned that life can be very hard, painful, and disappointing at times. I choose joy today not because everything is or ever will be perfect, but because I have grace and mercy from my Father.

When I returned to Oklahoma, I was heartsick. I had to hibernate for a few days. I could not even attend church. It really hit me hard that I had not seen them and they were not going to be a part of my life. It was really over. I was thankful to have a compassionate Christian counselor. She helped me tremendously.

I had so many questions. Was I looking for something that was never there and was impossible? I was hoping to recreate that mother child relationship, but that was impossible. Will I always have this feeling of separation from my son? I have sad memories of being a part of carrying him and being attached. He has no memories of that. I have thought about him almost every day. He may not have done that. I know I must forgive myself and move on. Regrets don't serve any purpose. It's amazing how a stranger can be a big part of my story—someone who came into my life and changed it forever!

> *Psalm 57: 1-3 Be gracious to me, O God, be gracious to me, For my soul takes refuge in you; And in the shadow of your wings I will take refuge Until destruction passes by. I will cry out to God Most High, To God who accomplishes all things for me. He will send from heaven and save me; He reproaches him who tramples upon me. God will send forth His loving kindness and His truth.*

I choose to be grateful for the answers God gave for my prayers about Doug through the years. I know He led me to North Carolina to meet and get to know my son and his family. I am thankful for the opportunity even though it does not seem to be a good situation right now. I am content with having met my son. I feel whole and complete. I think back on my life and see that My Heavenly Father has always been there. There were many times I failed, but He never will. I know I am good, whatever the outcome.

*Psalm 103:2 May I never forget the good things He has done for me.*

Oklahoma is known for tornadoes. One late night in May I awoke to the sound of my cell phone alert. I thought it was a flood warning because we had received a lot of rain in the past few days. It was actually a tornado warning. I checked the weather on TV and then went to my closet with pillows. It was pretty scary. My thoughts went to Doug. What if something happened to me and he did not know how I was doing and how I felt toward him with everything that had happened? The storm blew over and I was fine except for no electricity the rest of the night. The next day I sent him a text. I told him about the storm. I told him that even though we no longer had a relationship and were not connected, I do love him. I said that I was fine, trusting God and have accepted the way things turned out. He said he knew and that he loved me too. That was comforting.

\* \* \* \* \* \* \*

God did an amazing thing in September of 2018. He called Zack and his family to Oklahoma to serve at my church, South Tulsa Baptist Church. It has been phenomenal to have them so close. I get to see them every Sunday and Wednesday and other days as well.

God blesses me with them every day. I have two beautiful granddaughters and three handsome grandsons. It is heartwarming to see them run to greet me at church. It has been great to share holidays, birthdays, and the recent baptism of my six year old grandson. I have seen my son baptize three of his children and look forward to seeing the other two come to know the Lord as well.

I have been able to spend time with them on holidays such as Mother's Day and birthdays. Charlyanne planned a surprise party for Zack on his fortieth birthday. He never suspected and was totally surprised. It was so much fun helping her plan the surprise party and spend time with family and friends.

I get to see the kids on their birthdays as well. It is fun to see their faces light up when I give them birthday gifts. Charlyanne has texted me several times to go shopping with her. It is great to spend time with her and talk. We don't usually do that with all the kids around! So blessed to have them close.

I am so thankful to my South Tulsa Church Family. They have lovingly welcomed Zack and his family. Every week, several people from my church family will come up to me and tell me what a wonderful family I have. A church family is a blessing indeed! You must get a church family if you don't have one. You are welcome to join us at South Tulsa Baptist Church.

Zack is a talented songwriter. He has written many songs. The words to a song he wrote below really speak to how God is with us during the storms of life.

*Calmness*
*I won't fear tomorrow,*
*I will trust and follow.*
*Through the darkest shadows,*
*You are here with me.*

*Wanda S. Hudson*

*There's a calmness that sees me through,*
*When I get scared and I look to you.*
*There's a river that won't run dry.*
*You're life to me and it's flowing on the inside.*
*Your love awakens me, calling me out beyond what*
*I can see.*
*And I'll move with You.*
*Jesus, I'll move with You.*

*When this burden is heavy,*
*Too much for me to carry,*
*And when I am feeling weary,*
*You will lighten me.*

*CCLI License #184248 Zack Hudson*

# *Closing Thoughts*

Today, I know God is my strength. Today, I am much better, mostly healed with a few bad days here and there. A memory will pop in my head and I relive some of the good times with Doug and his family and miss those days. God's grace and mercy are with me always. God knows my heart as only He can know.

I could be angry and bitter over this situation. I choose to be grateful and joyful because I know God loves me. He knows the outcome. He has the answers. He has assured me and is my Protector. I accept that I may not know why most of this happened. I trust that He is shielding me from things that would be too harmful to me. I don't need any more heartbreak.

God is sovereign. It is because of Him that I am here today, writing my story. He knew before I was born everything that would happen. He knows what is in my future. He is already there.

> *Psalm 139; 15-16: You know me inside and out, you know every bone in my body; You know exactly how I was made, bit by bit, how I was sculpted from nothing into something. Like an open book, you watched me grow from conception to birth; all the stages of my life were spread out before you, the days of my life all prepared before I'd even lived one day.*

I do love Doug and his family. They are important to me. I don't know what else to do regarding them. Was it too much to expect a lasting relationship? Did I get too close and they were not ready for that? Did we try to put each other in a position that neither of us was ready to embrace? Did they not like my boundaries? Could I have been more compromising? I did a lot for them, but maybe it was overwhelming. I was very generous to them. I wanted to do whatever I could to help them. I let them use my car when they had car trouble and when I was out of town. There were other similar situations where I helped them as well. I acknowledge I was leading with my heart a lot.

I could play this what if game for a long time! I have to accept that I may never know what happened. Some days I feel hopeful that this situation will get resolved and some days I do not care. Some days I want a good resolution and some days I am fine. I recognize that they probably moved on long ago and this is not an issue for them today.

That is a hurtful reality to accept because I thought things were better than they really were. Doug and his family may be totally unaware how deeply this has affected me. I have not talked to them about this situation at all. It does not look as if I will be talking to them anytime soon.

I was never really sure of my role in their family. Perhaps I should have slowly been integrated into their lives. I feel like we rushed into things and did not talk things out. I was hoping for an open, honest relationship but don't think that ever happened. Today I realize that I never really felt like myself with them. I was who they thought I should be. I also wondered what their motivation was for finding me. We never really talked about that either. They seemed to just put me in their family and accept me. It was like I had always been a part of their family. I wanted it to be so perfect that I accepted whatever happened. I opened my heart, but that was not enough. We really all needed more time to adjust. We all have struggles we can't face. I may have just brought too much into their lives. I admit that I did see warning signs, but I chose to ignore them. It is a hard situation to confront. They may have seen warning signs as well. Sometimes life is just more than we can handle.

I wanted this so strongly that I really believed nothing could go wrong. I never thought it would be like this. When everything fell apart, I could not see it or accept it. Today I have no choice but to accept and move on with my life. I have to be done for now. I am no longer sad or hurt, just done.

I have learned that I cannot recreate that mother-child relationship. It was a bond that was severed when we were separated. It will never be whole again. I know that a reunion, while amazing and exciting, will not erase the reality of that broken bond. I feel like I have spent my life hoping for something that will never happen. I also know that God is making things right the way He has planned. With everything that has happened, I know God is faithful. I look ahead to the future, so thankful for the many blessings in my life. He is always working in our lives for our good.

I know my story has some sad, depressing and dreary stuff. There have been many heartbreaking days. Through it all, I know that God was there. He was, is and will always be with me. I rejoice today at all my Father has carried me through. He has lifted me, comforted me, and redeemed me. I trust Him even though things have not been resolved as I would like them to be. He has revealed more of Himself to me through my disappointments. He has proven Himself over and over to me. I have changed for the better through my experience. God brought courage and strength.

As I have been writing, the wounds open once again. Sometimes while I am at my computer, I see myself lying in the dark delivery room, cold and alone. Those wretched thoughts and questions haunt me once again. I pray, and He brings me healing. This book has brought real healing to my heart. I think it is the last phase of my healing process. God's love makes it bearable. Everything happens in God's timing.

One of my favorite verses is written below.

> *Ecclesiastes 3;11 He has made everything beautiful in its time.*

I do not know what the future holds with Doug and his family. It has been over two years since I have seen or talked to him and his family on the phone. We may never be close again. I choose to love them even though I may never see them again or have any kind of relationship with them. God knew I needed to know about Doug, if only for a short time. I know God puts people in our lives exactly when they are needed. His timing is perfect.

I have reread my journal posts from five years ago when this all started. It does not seem real now. I know it happened but it seems like forever ago. My prayer today is to love them. I can show kindness. It does not depend on them accepting my love. In my humanness, at times I just want to walk away and say I am done. I am so thankful that Jesus never gave up on me, even when He was dying on the cross for me and for you.

> *John 16:33 Be courageous! I have conquered the world.*

CPSIA information can be obtained
at www.ICGtesting.com
Printed in the USA
FSHW011156260420